I0164303

THE LITTLE BOOK OF LONGER POEMS

by

Rev. David E. Clarke

Rev. David E. Clarke
P.O. 82
Ashville, Ohio 43103

Published by FWB Publications
Columbus, Ohio

FWB

Rev. David E. Clarke

DEDICATION

To those of so long ago
To those so long apart
To those of a time more slow
To those having both soul and heart
They of a time when there was right
They of a time when the path was clear
They of a time under the Lord's might
They of a time of both laughter and tear
I follow those of this different pace
I follow the old and out of date
I follow in line toward His grace
I follow, though I am one born late

Mostly to my Lord and Savior

Ho Kurios Mou Kai Ho Theos Mou

ACKNOWLEDGEMENTS

I thank my brother and sister-in-law, Len and Linda Clarke. In my life, they have helped in various and many ways.

Thank you Len for the title of this work.

To my daughter Myrriah Elyse. My joy and light.

PREFACE

I have reconciled myself to the fact that I am not a modern person. My mind and soul are wired in a way more appropriate to the Middle Ages and before the supposed Enlightenment. So be it.

These poems are not for the modern reader. The verses presuppose that the Lord reigns, as He does. I like the Apostle Paul be in Christ and He crucified and He resurrected. The modern reader may find these simple works jaded and works out of time.

Some of them have been published in my previous books and are so noted. I desired to have under one title my longer poems and this is the rationale of this little book.

TABLE OF CONTENTS

The Little Book of Longer Poems

TWILIGHT'S CONFESSION

At cliff's ledge
Peril seemed before
Standing by the edge
The unknown in store
Dark winds blew
The numinous gathered about
My future seemed dark
I gave no fearful shout
Resources were none
Nothing ahead
All light all but gone
Loneliness instead
A stark barren place
Beckoning with eerie sound
A place seemingly without grace
A forbidding hideous ground
Fear raised its scream within
No path ahead just the fall
Wind's blow, lightning's din
Driving me to their call

Deep within my soul
Knowledge began to rise
Only forward and off could I go
What future to find?
Turning and looking back
A steep path I had trod
Finishing high and here
Bowing to mortality's prod
So much I did not know
Was my path to end here?
Having travelled the hard life
A short time left to appear
Darkness began to give way
The wind calmed a bit
The lightning abated
My mind became more fit
I looked all about
Up and down and all around
I gazed craving all I could see
Standing on this high ground

The eerie ebbing away
I knew where I was
Sense came amid the sway
My end was coming as it does
I looked over the deep drop
Wasn't the river the final path?
Either way, a time of change
Short-lived for the prior wrath
Here I found himself
A million questions, but no time
I shook a bit to my core
An absence of meter or rhyme
A time to look
A time to feel
A time to reflect
A time to heal
A paradox rose
Things either and or
Answers to my questions
I was entering a different door

From where I had journeyed
I looked back and down
Peering over the edge
My thoughts ever more sound
Atop here I would know
Questions finding an end
Life long, but very short
Where to begin?
Still gazing behind
Viewing down the drop
I saw and was amazed
Looking at my life's crop
What I had grown
What I had done
What I had hidden
Away from the sun
What others would never know
What others would never find
My deeds hidden and covered
My deeds of the darkest kind

I was shocked at the scope
Of the revelation that was to be
Every bad thing arose
Few good works to see
The movie of my life
From birth until my end
Rose and flooded my soul
Where to begin?
I could not hide
I could not cower
I could not justify
Not having the power
All I could do was watch
Observing my pitiful state
To have fallen so short
Nothing worthy to this date
From birth to small child
This babe under attack
Surrounded by monsters
Trying to devour and distract

But a shielding light
Surrounded the heart of this child
Keeping the dangers at bay
This child's soul was kept mild
The roaring and the screams
Of those against this one
Were apart from my soul
The light was sent from the Son
A protection was given
A sheltering from the storm
This little one's defense
By the mercy of the Lord
Protection was on the inside
Of this wee child so mild
The monsters were so cruel
The monsters were so wild
I looked back at the scene
From the top of the mount
Seeing through the crimes
Eternally covered by the fount

The scene now had changed
This child was more grown
The shielding light was gone
This child's choices were my own
My mind was bent
Not knowing the norm
My mind was afloat
Riding through the storm
The monsters still came
The crimes still were done
I found I was guilty
I had become a monstrous son
Crimes against the youth
Crimes which were my own
Hurting the world about
A dismal time was known
I thought only of my needs
Corrupt and bent to the core
All I wanted I grabbed
Leaving myself and others sore

The monsters sired another
The monsters had a kin
Not seeing the normal of life
This lad falling more in sin
Soon I was growing and grown
Through this and forward in time
All through my corruption and distance
All away from the Son's rhyme
Now that time from the cliff's edge
I knew who held my hand
For all my faults, sins, and hurts
He ushered this sinner to His land
Instead of a fall from the past
Now a simple step to the land before
Past the cliff and river that loomed
To an eternal serene shore
Twilight's confession was of this day
Such a failure I had been
But my weakness gave up due His sway
He overcame all weakness and sin.

7-2018

A DIFFERENT PATH

The light
The might
I moved from the main
Creating a strain
The Lord my preeminent sight

They push for more
From their store
They say do the norm
Avoid the storm
But I have a different chore

To amass like they
To do what they say
Do not think old
But grab the gold
Listen to their modern bray

I reach for Him
Forget their whim
Turn back the clock
Anchor to His dock
The material will only dim

They travel too far down their road
Allowing a selfish goad
Ignoring the right
Becoming a fallen knight
Absorbing a selfish load

Not for me
Only He can I see
He is my Lord
I speak His sword
It is all I can be

I have turned my back
I considered their aim, their lack
I have counted the cost
I choose not to be lost
But there comes their attack

I walk the old way
Against their modern sway
I look to His path
I am relieved from His wrath
Coming in His day

They rush to the fore
Coveting the more
They want
The material is their flaunt
Rushing past me to an opposite shore

I push back
From an inevitable attack
So many of them
My number so slim
My number so slack

They say we are right
Look at our might
You are few
We must be true
You are a blight

I stand
I can
He is
Nothing amiss
I must be a man

He is true
Though the number is few
His way will grow
To those who wish to know
His way is due

The numbers belie
The common thought makes you die
Apart from Him
Covered with sin
I cannot be their ally

I must stand
I will, I can
Suffering their barb
Suffering their harm
I see the eternal land

On and on
They say you must belong
Not to old ways
Not like in now gone days
Only in the 'me' can you be strong

Of course they lie
They see the short and then they die
They cast away and far
The eternal divine star
To Him I'll draw nigh

I am bonded and sure
In Him I am secure
Thought by them to be a fool
But I cannot be their tool
I will avoid and ignore their lure

Soon the day will loom
As the bride I will see the Groom
He will call me from this land
And on distant glory I will stand
Choosing life lieu the doom

Immersed in His love as a bath
I will not see the wrath
Of those who chose the wrong
Whose greed rose so strong
I chose a differing path

7-28-2015

-HE GIVES-

He gives me love
    He gives me peace
He is my Dove
    He causes my longing to cease
He sees me through
    He lifts me up
He loves me and you
    He drank the bitter cup
I thank Him for a handshake and a smile
    I thank Him for a church who is a friend
I thank Him for a hug from my child
    I thank Him for an eternity to begin
He sees me:
    through my failures
    through the last mile
    through my successes
    through the final trial
I thank Him for daughters and son
    a teacher
A prayer
    my preacher
My best friend
    others now gone
Those who love me
    even when I am wrong
My job
    my call
My poems
    He is my all

The air
    the hills
The paycheck
    the bills
A band of community
    and fellowship there
A family that loves me
    they really care
During my distresses
    when I am at my less
When I am not together
    when I am at my best
He carried me
    and has for so long
He carries me
    when I am not strong
In the desert
    across the mountain high
In the valley
    when I cannot try
The sunshine
    the rain
The gentle winds
    the waving grain
His truth
    His grace
Loving for the now
    and His future place

His eternal plan
 He gives to me
He helps this poet man
 He allows me to see
His salvation He imparts
 He restores my soul
He, my soul does save
 He sets heaven as my goal
He, my provision remains
 He permits a roof over me
He, my health maintains
 He allows me to be
He, my children returned
 He heals my lonely heart
He is my source that burns
 He loved me from the start
He gives me food
 He gives me garb
He gives me breath
 He keeps me from harm
He gives me my bed

 He gave me my son
He gave me my daughters' laugh
 my, they are such fun
He keeps during my travail
 He gives me my pace
He keeps me from strife
 He gives me his grace

He kept me during my poverty
 He keeps me during my gain
He kept me during my lack
 He gives ease from the strain
He helps me:
 Through My Tear
 Through My Weakness
 Through My Fear
 Through Me Meekness
 Through My Low
 Through My High Times
 Through The Blow
 Through The Barb Unkind
He's always there
 He's always my friend
He always cares
 He washes away my sin
He gave me a work to do
 He lets His light shine
He always stays true
 He gives me His rhyme[1]

5-03

---

[1] "He Gives," was first published in Eclectic Essays, FWB Publishing.
c. 2011

-THE CHRISTMAS –

-From a Manger to a Divine Throne-

His birth in a manger low
To a divine throne He will sit upon
He comes from Heaven to dwell below
Both acts prove He is God's Son
In His glory that is coming
In His glory that is soon
In His glory that transcends
Both the sun and the moon
He will come and sit down
He will reign and settle all
He will rule all that is around
When He fills the temple hall
Majesty will live with frailty
Love will rule those in need
Justice coupled with charity
Messiah to answerers of His heed
God's glory made mortal
To go back to Father above
Then return from Heaven's portal
To complete the Father's perfect love

-The Beginnings-

This story of a long time ago
When mankind chose to lose his way
God decided upon grace
Enabling man the option not to stray
God had a glorious noble thought
A design of a divine loving plan
Sent to each and every one
God would send Himself as a man
Through many long separated years
He gave His message and promise
To all who would hear and listen
Of His plan that is never amiss
From one beginning He gave man life
Though all chose to sin and disobey
Now a second beginning to end the strife
So man could span the gulf and pray
Tonight is the time and the star rides high
For God breathes as a mortal man
To bring peace to all in a lost world
Reconciling all through His free plan

-The Divine in Bethlehem-

The town of King David, a town some low
A town where God's glory soon will glow
God's grace will draw His first breath
A royal one who conquers death
In birth, He will so humbly begin
A poor little babe to overcome sin
He was, is and forever will be divine
Tonight, tonight begins His mortal time
The star guides and angels are bending low
A town, this town now radiantly glows

-Divine and Holy-

He is Christ, the Chosen One
He is the Begotten, God's only Son
He, His mortality will begin
A man who will never know sin
He is divine and holy is He
He is born for you and me

-Comes the Shepherds-

The cool night envelopes the shepherds there
Something is different and stirring in the air
God's angel has said that a miracle is to be
A savior born this day for them to see
Leaving their flock to journey there
Leaving their world for one who cares
All their lives, traditions and lore
Have this day manifested in one to adore
They come to a stable, dark and dank
They come to see the babe and God to thank

-Comes the Kings-

They are kings, the Magi and wise
They travel far to see with their own eyes
This gift from God given to man
They travel from a very distant land
They bring gifts of great value
But God's gift reigns most true
They thank God for giving them the days
To come and see and give this babe praise

-Messiah, Messiah-

The babe here is the one anointed
This babe here is the one appointed
To restore and allow every man
To come to the Father and to stand
Judge Him not from the birth in a manger low
Judge His Lordship the Father bestows
He is the Christ, the Messiah and this means
He is the Savior to those who have seen
Messiah, Messiah truly the chosen One
Christos, Christos the only begotten Son
Savior, Savior worthy of our laud
My Lord, my Lord the only Son of God

-A Birth for All-

His birth is for you and for me
His birth is for all who believe
The Christmas then and to this day
Allows us the right to pray
Through manger and cross man He will lift
God gave Jesus for as our Christmas gift
His cross, tomb and resurrection day
Allows us the right to pray
His plan from the first to the last
Upon the Lord man's hope may cast
Around the manger and for all eternity
His provision is made for you and me.[2]

11-93

---

[2] "The Christmas," was first published in, Eclectic Essays, FWB
Publishing. c.2011

A JUST QUEST

The valley so very, very still
A dale of dying flesh and will
Soon so many hurt on the ground they lie
Soon so many more prostrate they die
There the enemy, my soul felt the chill

I with my friends
Stood this ground again
Armored with our nerve
Our resolve and our verve
Perhaps our last battle to begin

The valley formed as a cone
Covered with grass and stone
Soon more with body and blood
Overshadowing the flowering bud
The crush of the mind and the bone

My friends and allies stood the by
Perhaps our last battle under the Lord's sky
True and valiant they were
Ignoring the fallen one's lure
Willing for a quest to stand and die

My friends were given to me
My friends from Him came to be
They stood their ground
Their message sound
He through them for all to see

I saw Justice so tall
Standing with Mercy in answering the call
Faith from the start
Grace gave all His heart
Prudence ne'er a lull

Charity with His love
Hope came from the Dove
Peace came to fight the war
All for Him faced whatever in store
They and I stood for the Son

Others followed their noble lead
Others as soldiers obeying His heed
We formed a core
To withstand the sore
To fight the fight, to do the deed

O'er the top of the hill
Came a foe breaking the still
Encircling around
With their deafening sound
Wanted to maim, to kill

Their numbers large
Readying their charge
We seemed so few
A noble, but a lesser crew
Awaiting blood's baptism sparge

The horde came at the run
Pulling their sword, arming their gun
Lust for blood
Their hatred's flood
Would our stand be done

The battle's haze
A journey through a hard maze
The chaos
The battler's pathos
A hit, a stab, a fighter's daze

I felt a pain
I gave to the strain
No longer whole
My pain did grow
The grave may be my gain

My plight, so long
Now weak when first so strong
With troubled breath where to begin
I fought and ran and fought again
Until struck down and hit about and along

The dark swept about
My spirit dull and with doubt
But I grabbed His mind
To be of His kind
From down deep I heard my shout

I must stay the course
I must make Him my resource
Whatever the day
I will not stray
From His cause I will not divorce

Sun's rays rise
Falling on weathered eyes
Another day
Here I lay
A breath, my surprise

From my posit prone
I felt no joy and so alone
I gazed about in my lowly state
Oh, to live or to cross death's gate
Hurting from blows of steel and stone

Growing warm
An aching form
I did not die
And still I lie
Surviving the storm

I looked as I lay
From two battered eyes of dismay
The hills above and misted and green
A hue now dull when once so keen
Could I rise or must I stay

The wrath of battle done
Victors and vanquished under the sun
I rose to a knee
I looked about me
I felt for sword and gun

I gazed my fellows fallen
Lost and gone still I was calling
My friend and also foes
Brought low with enmity and blows
So much, so appalling

The wreckage of the cause
Reeling still in my pause
Where are they
Did they not stay
A confusing lull

A few had fled
The many. died and bled
I sought only to rise
I stood and looked with misting eyes
So many gone in my stead

I must travel the more
I must face whatever in store
I stand this ground
I must not embrace the coward's hound
So much loss, so much gore

I turned my head in wheel
Not sure what to feel
A gasp, a pant
My world not straight, but aslant
I must stand and never kneel

The battle long
I tried to be strong
The foe
So low
So very hard and wrong

I had stood and fought
The battle wrought
An arduous time
With no redeeming rhyme
Life's reprieve somehow I bought

My cause
My loss
Not to be
As long as I see
I stand evil's dross

Was I alone?
A nagging pain's echo of a groan
A buzzing, a nagging
Just hurt no bragging
I heard from inside me a moan

I looked about me
To see what I could see
The noble laid
The noble stayed
Seemingly gone, having paid the whole fee

A moment to the left and right
The arising of might
The lords once again began to move
Life began to loom
My day overcoming my night

To my right Justice again stood
Next to him Mercy again could
Faith so true
Grace who all knew
Prudence did good

Charity rose in love
Hope displayed his Dove
Peace returned once gone for a time
The lords resounded their rhyme
All remained with the Son

I felt such peace
My lords, my friends, my release
From a hard fear
With a victory tear
They stood in their deeds

The vanquished lay about
The horror, the doubt
The warring sin
The absence of the din
The cost, the count

Had we won
Were we done
We stood their charge
We stood so large
Our only and all for the Son

The foe had come o'er the hill
Toward us to maim and kill
They reveled in their task
Obscured behind their evil mask
We soon heard their dying shrill

The lords, the crowd and finally I
Stayed to thwart the horde, willing to die
Evil in that group so vile
We would run the last mile
We would give all in this battle nigh

They thought themselves best
We gave evil a rest
We fought for the One
We fought for the Son
We had rallied to the test

We beheld the cause
We calmed in seeing a pause
A hiatus in this sway
A light shown bright as day
He is and He was and nary a lull

When we stood facing our foe
In our midst was His glow
A light so bright
Demonstrating divine might
He stood there with sword and bow

Our Lord throughout the dale
Our Lord and around us would prevail
He armed His men
He let us begin
He went with us into the travail

When we fell
He was there so death to quell
He took our hand
He let us stand
His victory, His tale

For the lords came from Him
I and the force allowed to begin
All we are
The earth and the stars
Reflect Him never to dim

The war was won
By the ever obedient Son
The quest
The test
The plan now done

We stand for the Lord
All of us via His sword
His true way
His coming day
He has cut the fallen chord

Let us praise
His perfect days
So complete
His power replete
His loving and righteous ways

He forever will stand
He redeems all the land
Whatever we are
Reflect His star
All the saved of man

1-2016

LOVE'S FINAL SCENE

I look back with older eyes
So few the wins or the prize
I see her once more
I love her from my core
Life has went on many years
At times I have shed tears
My failures, my doubts
My attempts, my shouts
Never with her the victor to be
Though it is her the love I see
Could she have gleaned
Upon her love I have leaned
Once again from older eyes
Rejected from her prize

When I was young and strong
I thought I could do no wrong
I saw first her from afar
The first sight left me ajar
I could but stumble
Words were a mumble
I felt an unworth
Though I felt a new birth
All before I knew was less
I knew she was my best
Her form and her face
Shone with true grace
I was young and thought myself strong
The decades passed and I was wrong

Still she stayed in my mind
Life was life and sometimes unkind
Day and then another day
Passed the years as they may
I tried to live without her
Every now and then I felt her stir
I left the common and walked away
I left our town and I hoped her sway
I tried to find another love
But inevitably I felt an inevitable shove
Not that she ever pushed the goad
I had no answer for love's heavy load
Her spirit and grace drove deep in me
Forcing that alone I must be

She herself did nothing to me
Still I knew I had to flee
She was not at fault
I was just in a stupor caught
I still am not sure she completely knew
I know she never gave me a clue
It was all me and never her
Still in my love I found no cure
So apart I must live my life
The only path away from strife
Away and alone
Caves of heart and not of stone
I am assuming this path for me
I live alone for it must be

I write this word in a final scene
I write this note not to be mean
I know she lived the life she had
I know she was good and not bad
It was my heart
From the start
A failing time
I had the bad rhyme
It perhaps could not be
That in this way she could see me
I was broke and had such lack
I fell under this impossible attack
In the end, it may not seem fair
In this end, I still love and care

I don't think I will write of her again
But she is in my heart now as then
Let me just say lady my fair
Lady I still do care
When heart's last beat comes to me
Your face and all I will see
Many say I have a wasted life
Never to love and to live in unrequited strife
But I still see your face and all
For many years and in my pall
I can only say that I have known love
Never finished, but still above
To not is to be the more sad
To love like I did is never bad.

2-1-2016

FOR THE BRIDE, FOR THE WORLD

The pain I go through
And the labor I do
I'll understand as ne'er before
By the peaceful regal shore
When we marry God's Son
When this hard life is done
He'll wipe grief away
At the wedding meeting day
The loss I feel here
With the sadness and tear
No more will I feel
My all and all He will heal
I'll ask the how and why
For me, He chose to die
My heartaches down I'll lay
At the wedding meeting day
This life I'll no longer care
His way I will share
My invitation given to me
When He died at Calvary
Unworthy to be there
I'll join the grand affair
"Come on up," I'll hear Him say
At the wedding meeting day
At the wedding meeting day
With my Lord I'll ever stay
When I lay my burdens down
He'll hand to me a crown
I'll give it back to Him

For He took away my sin
With my Lord I'll ever stay
At the wedding meeting day
He will come, He will come
Not for all, but a chosen some
Ne'er this world to be of again
No more pain, no more sin
O'er the clouds I will behold
The One who died long ago
I'll see the Son of God so near
I'll gaze at the Lamb so dear
He will come for me in the sky
He will come but not to die
His word spoke of why He came
For me, His bride, the very same
I will fly up to my King
Forever His praises to sing
I will fly up to my King
Ne'er to feel death's futile sting
At the wedding meeting day
With my Lord I'll ever stay
When I lay my burdens down
He'll hand me a crown
I'll give it back to Him
For He took away my sin
With my Lord I'll ever stay
At the wedding meeting day
The bride will go home
But the world stays on
To finish the Lord's divine plan
A time of worry for remaining man

Troubling trials of the worst kind
The selfishness of 'me' the common mind
But the world is not lost
For His reconciliation paid the cost
The world will be redeemed
And divine lightning will been seen
From bursting clouds He will appear
Away with sorrow, away with tear
In His day, the chore is done
All is His when He does come
From the sky the world will behold
His return with a crown of gold
The Lamb will come, oh what a sight
He will come with power and might
He will reign and sit on His throne
He will rule and lead His own
Zion's mount will split and the river will flow
His truth will abound and sin will go
Clouds will remove in start of His coming
Birds will light and cease their calling
Voices will stop in awe of the Son
The world will rest, travail is done
Trumpets will blare to announce His word
Hosts will sing for He is the Lord
Angels will shout, "The King is here!"
Pain will resign with the tear
Corruption will cease, the world's birth pangs are o'er
For in His kingdom, perfection is the norm
All fear will end not like now
In His kingdom all knees will bow
He will come and the ideal will be

The Lord of all and all will see
He will come for His throne
The Lord of all will come with His own
His peace and love forever will flow
His restoration complete and bestowed
A bride claimed and married in His love
A world restored by the divine eternal Dove.[3]

10-26-00

---

[3] The Poem, "For The Bride, For The World," was first published in, <u>Concerning the Christ,</u> FWB Publishing, c. 2011.

A COMING TIME

A crushing chide
A rising tide
Soon the blow
Evil will grow
Good is bad
Forever more the sad
They chose in themselves to dwell
Never again to be well
Their good they throw away
In evil they choose to stay
Their view of their own
Within hearts of stone
My God
They chose not to laud
Away from us they cry
Come our way or you must die
An evil here
A sigh, a tear
An evil there
They no longer care
Good is bad and bad is good
They do wrong and not as they should
Me and more me
They cry for all to see
He above and others don't matter
Only the new, only this latter
Some say only a craze
Others only a phase

But I see an overall plan
A final throb in the land
For in evil mind
They think not in kind
They should look and seek
They should repent and be meek
They think and know in part
They must put on the good heart
For a greater good will grow
For a greater plan will show
Good even with terror everywhere
Will prove the Lord is still there
When they say no
His light will grow
A light
In the night
Showing the more
In the middle of darkness' core
To stand the stand
In a vile evil land
Will stop the curse
And show his verse
For no matter evil scope
The Lord will give His hope
Hold to his hand
During a dark land
Some soon day
For those who do not stray
A light will rise
In what once were dark skies
A new day will come
In the fullness of the Son

Evil will pass
Along with all its cast
Hurt and pain
The straining strain
Will fall and go
And disappear in a washing glow
For He is the one
He is the Son
He will over throw
He will cast low
All that is not
All that is rot
All not of Him
All that is sin
All that is curt
All that does hurt
Then only will be His love
Demonstrating the Father above
Oh come the day when this is done
Forever the day of the Son.
For it will be His rhyme
Finally in a coming time.

2-1-2016

The Hunting Trip[4]

In my youth so many years ago,
   my brother and I bravely would travail
In an unfamiliar land and we would know
   a hunter's prize and a hunter's tale

We were south at the family home
   of Uncle Len and Aunt Gil
But we were bound to travel and roam
   we would for our goal quest until

A hunter's success we would glean
   from those Tennessean trees
We would not return nor be seen
   for mighty hunters we would be

Our family was there kind and true
   for they knew our desperate need
From some a warning and a hoorah from a few
   and Cousin Deb with a 'be careful' plea

We left their home with some aid
   three great and noble hounds
We would spend both night and day
   and run until our game we found

---

[4] The Poem, The Hunting Trip, was first published, "Eclectic Essays."
Published by FWB Publishing, c. 2011.

We scurried through the fields
   our trained dogs anxious in our tow
Neither gun nor knife did we wield
   nor did we need arrows or bow

Our wits and dogs would be all
   that we boy hunters would need
For we were able to stand tall
   those dogs would bid our heed

We went left and then to the right
   over this fence and then that one
My, oh my we were soon a sight
   we now walked and could not run

We jumped another fence
   and had a frightening start
There was a brahma bull so tense
   we stopped and so did our heart

Our hounds hit the brakes
   and shook their muddled heads
I think they knew of our mistake
   I think they feared they were dead

That fear shared by me and my bro
   this once proud and eager crew
Fell into a funk, a sadness so low
   there was only one thing to do

We grabbed the dogs and bid adieu
   we ran for the fence huffing and puffing
Over the fence our hounds we threw
   for the bull would stomp them to stuffing

We turned and looked at the enemy there
   soon we could tell he would charge
Len and I cleared the fence with no flair
   that bull was way too large

After our escape, we turned and saw
   the bull's face seemed sad it appeared
The bull snorted and he seemed in a pall
   at his failed try and seemed to shed a tear

Len and I stood and looked about
   our dogs were in great disarray
Len gave out with a mighty shout
   we could not let them stray

What would we say to Gil and Len
   to cousins Pat, Dianne and Debbie there
If these dogs were never seen again
   after they were placed in our care

Dad and Mom were waiting at Len's home
   if in our charge and task we feel short
Would they be mad if we came back alone
   would they yell or would they be curt

We both knew that this could not be
    we ran and coaxed and called around
After a time, we had regained all three
    but we knew we were on strange ground

The hounds were anxious and so were we
    the day was long past and we wanted ease
For our hunting trip was a flop for all to see
    Len and I just wanted some relief

We looked around and started to roam
    we walked and went this and that way
In truth we didn't know the way home
    this trip had become a long lost day

We heard the sound of cars going by
    what a busy road we both thought
We grabbed the dogs after a great try
    what new misadventures had we wrought

Chased by a bull and leaping many a fence
    we almost lost Uncle Len's dogs, all three
Now we were racked from any remaining sense
    would this strange road a final injury be

With what strength we had that remained,
    we cleared the brush line by the road
The dogs leapt and pulled with a strain
    Len and I tired of this increasing load

What road was this, where could we be
  we did not remember a road there
There was nothing familiar that we could see
  the road was busy, we had to take care

Three antsy dogs and two boys in a pout
  a strange and comical tale to be retold
Suddenly a car stopped and we heard a shout
  my Mom spoke with a happy ringing scold

She and Dianne in a car had sought us out
  they would relieve us from our plight
We were bolstered by her informing shout
  but we must have been quite a sight

We endured the laughs about our day
  I guess all boys have had this sort of thing
The day Len and I with a pack went astray
  and a mean old bull proved he was king

5-03-01

THE HOLY BIBLE

The Old Testament[5]

Genesis, the book of beginnings
  begin your work in me O Lord
  permit me to live in your court
Exodus, the book of names
  write your name in my soul
  allow your light in me to grow
Numbers, the book of wanderings
  let me wander in your land
  renew me to be a holy man
Leviticus, the book of the called
  call me Lord and I will go
  teach me your path to know
Deuteronomy, the book of words
  write your word in my heart
  guide my quest from the start
Joshua, the book of a mighty leader
  teach me your holy word
  let that be what others have heard
Judges, the book of a time of shame
  keep me in my pathway
  fortify me O Lord I pray
Ruth, the book of love
  help me love as you loved me O Lord
  outfit me with your divine sword

---

[5] The Old Testament poem was first published in, "Eclectic Essays."
FWB Publishing. c. 2011.

First Samuel, the book of change
    mold me to reflect your grace
    permit me to live before your face
Second Samuel, the book of David
    let me cling to you
    let me to be a servant true
First Kings, the book of Solomon
    let your wisdom encircle my state
    let your righteousness hedge my estate
Second Kings, the book of war
    make me strong
    I wish to your cause to belong
First Chronicles, the book of Judah
    make me of your regal line
    fill me with your Spirit divine
Second Chronicles, the book of judgment
    adopt me into your royal family
    craft a loyal slave of me
Ezra, the book of the return
    return me to your place sublime
    enable me to be more kind
Nehemiah, the book of the second return
    give your peace to me
    demonstrate it for others to see
Esther, the book of a queen's love
    let me care for everyone around
    let your clarion call sound

Job, the book of faith during trouble
    save me from the trouble of this life
    remove from me evil's strife
Psalms, the book of praise
    let me praise your name renown
    I will give you my worker's crown
Proverbs, the book of wisdom
    give me wisdom and love
    let me reflect you above
Ecclesiastes, the book of the preacher
    anoint me your message to speak
    I will always your presence seek
Song of Solomon, the book of the wife
    make and keep me your bride
    in your refuge, let me hide
Isaiah, the book of the evangelical prophet
    let me be meek
    never find me weak
Jeremiah, the book of the broken hearted prophet
    break my heart and take my pride
    never let me hear your chide
Lamentations, the book of the temple's fall
    keep me from failing you
    let me be faithful all the way through
Ezekiel, the book of the prophet of change
    change me into your image
    I want to view your holy visage
Daniel, the book of the prophet of visions
    give me a vision of your way
    I will trust you all my days

Hosea, the book of the prophet to Israel
    let me be faithful and wise
    let me to see through your eyes
Joel, the book of the prophet to Judah
    let me be receptive
    let me your life live
Amos, the book of the prophet of judgment
    judge me in my servant's lot
    remove from me any evil plot
Obadiah, the book of the prophet to Edom
    judge me loyal
    my King so royal
Jonah, the book of the first prophet to Nineveh
    grant me mercy in your judgment
    in your service, make me adamant
Micah, the book of the prophet to the south
    grant me purity
    please Lord use me
Nahum, the book of the second prophet to Nineveh
    keep me from wrath
    set me on your straight path
Habakkuk, the book of the prophet who questioned
    let me bow on my knee
    only you do I want to see
Zephaniah, the book of the prophet of your coming
    keep me in your day
    keep me on your way
Haggai, the book of the prophet of the rebuilding
    make me serve
    enable me to never swerve

Zechariah, the book of the encouraging prophet
    in all my ways and in all my days
    let me always your name praise
Malachi, the book of the prophet without compromise
    finish your work in me O Lord
    strengthen me to abide in your court

5-16-01

THE NEW TESTAMENT[6]

Matthew, the book of the King
    My King and my Lord
    The Messiah of Israel's accord
Mark, the book of the Servant
    Let me serve and give
    Through You I may live
Luke, the book of the Son of Man
    You came as the One
    The serving obedient Son
John, the book of the Son of God
    Forever was, will and is
    Your plan with nothing amiss
The Acts of the Apostles, the book of transitions
    The growth and the plan
    Lord's remedy to fallen man
Romans, the book of the grace of the Lord
    From the worst to the best
    A plan to reveal and to attest
First Corinthians, the book of correction
    So many apart and away
    Let me come and not stray
Second Corinthians, the book of Paul's authority
    Paul, called to lead and sow
    The gentile bride to grow

---

[6] The New Testament, was first published in, "Songs Without Music and Other Poems." FWB Publishing. c. 2015.

Galatians, the book of our freedom
    Leave the law and be free
    His grace, the price of liberty
Ephesians, the book of our heavenly call
    Gracious Lord my all in all
    Precious Lord guide me to stand tall
Philippians, the book of our exhortation in holiness
    Set me apart and keep me strong
    Help me not err or go wrong
Colossians, the book of the preeminent Christ
    No one could be before
    No one, but You divine Lord
First Thessalonians, the book of correcting console
    Hold to gracious truth and stay
    Hold fast against the tribulational sway
Second Thessalonians, the book of correcting comfort
    Let me grow during the strife
    Let me wait for You during this life
First Timothy, the book to be a faithful minister
    Let me stay the course and stand
    Watch over me and your given band
Second Timothy, the book to continue on
    Teach me and let me do the work
    Times are nearing which will hurt
Titus, the book of encouragement for strength
    Allow me to persevere against the falsity
    Permit me to work and stand and be
Philemon, the book of a slave and a master
    The master may be
    The slave is surely free

Hebrews, the book that Christ is better and best
 You are Lord above angels, fathers and law
 You are Lord first, last and above all
James, the book to the twelve tribes
 Strengthen me to be ready for the day
 Encourage me to work and never stray
First Peter, the book to bear our suffering
 My hope to be holy during the hard kind
 Suffering before the Lord's return time
Second Peter, the book showing the truth and false
 Let me rest in Your truth and not deny
 Let me beware of the evil apostate lie
First John, the book of fellowship
 Grant me to walk and obey Your love
 Pure and triumph through You, the Son
Second John, the book of pure steadfastness
 Always in the truth of You
 Shunning the lie always to be true
Third John, the book contrasting real and error
 Be true in godly generosity from the start
 Condemn the prideful and sinful heart
Jude, the book to guard against heresy
 Fallacy past, now and then
 Avoid the lie and the sin
The Revelation of Jesus Christ to John
  The seventieth week soon will come
 The kingdom of You, the glorious Son

07-2011

THE CLOUDS[7]

Do you see this base earth?
Do you see the way, the path?
Do you see the evil sway and turn?
Do you see the coming of the final wrath?

For a time, there was a clear light
A time for those who wanted to come
A time of grace and not of fearful fright
The gathering of the bride to the Son

That time is over and the 70th begins
A time to finish and claim the Divine's prize
A time to end man's enchantment with sin
A time to watch with watchful eyes

Look upon the skies above
Do you see here and there the clouds?
Now mortality lives in a world without love
And evil is roaming about and loud

The storm comes to earth
In a new way, but still very old
Bringing a pall for charity's dearth
Now all must walk the long hard road

---

[7] Words within this poem that are capitalized are words from Scripture
which glorify the Divine Triune God and the Lord's works.

The clouds above have differing hues
One smaller with red of menace and without peace
One regal, the Royal Blue
One, the White Cloud of noble relief

But another is so very dark
And wants to wrest away the rest
For he is evil, real and stark
He comes bringing evil's test

The Servant loyal leaves
Taking the bride to her Royal Groom
No restraint is left and evil is received
The dark cloud mightily looms

The hills and water and the valley ground
Groan and stir and labor so
For in travail they move all around
As greater evil upon all will grow

In time, there will be a perfect peace
But now the dark cloud boasts so loud
He brings hurt and pain and no relief
Such a burden rises from the dark cloud

A tremor there and a sway here
And his evil is moving all about
To bring his lies and brag and tears
His posturing and his arrogant shout

What he is no one can ever doubt
For his good is nowhere to be found
For he swaggers as he touts
That this is his earthly ground

No one remaining escapes his glove
For the earth and all that live
Are covered throughout, inside and above
With the menace that he gives

The White Cloud is still above
For he, the Father God is always there
But the dark cloud feels no love
He acts and does without any care

The Royal Blue Cloud can be seen
But most do not heed the Prince below
The evil is what the earth wants so keen
The evil stretches and bellows and grows

For the few that hold to the Prince
They sing and praise and stand fast
To an evil world they seem without sense
This new world will see the few won't last

The dark cloud will embrace the red
For they are part and parcel of each
They hover over the hurt and the dead
For red war is within their hungry reach

They move around and gather a crowd
They call and encourage a mob
They declare the earth theirs and are so proud
From the White Cloud, the earth they will rob

The majority of the earth gathers up
They want to follow the darker one
They prefer to drink from his bitter cup
Not honoring the Royal Prince Son

The darker cloud with evils galore
Will give to each their deadly pill
For a short time they will receive more
But in the end they will be killed

Do any still live for the good and just?
With such a dark foreboding way
Will any forsake this evil lust?
Will any stand tall in this evil day?

In the heavens above and away
Removed from this time of wrath
An assembly has happened quickly this day
Those who walked the Prince's path

The bride, the bride flew away
With the Servant Spirit back to home
The bride will be ready soon for the wedding day
The bride no more in mortality to roam

The Groom, the Head, the Royal Son
The Blue Cloud will account for the bride
Her conduct and what she has done
While walking for Him in her once life

Her work under judgment is done
Her time of judgment has come
What she has accomplished for the Son
Many pass the test; failure for some

Those of the bride that have the worth
Receive a rare and costly crown
For their works while on the earth
For their Groom, they lay their crowns down

Before the Lord they bow low
Their Head and their Groom
They all reside in His radiate glow
Their marriage for eternity will come soon

For the gleaning has happened and is complete now
The Royal Blue Cloud reigns supreme
Let the trumpet blow and sound so loud
The Royal Blue Cloud is King of kings

Their knowledge is made perfect
Their hearts full of His love
They are complete in His gift
Made total by God's perfect Dove

The trumpets readied are brought up high
The angelic clouds prepare their heavenly song
The bride is judged ready to draw nigh
A bride pure and chaste and righteously strong

The bride of many parts is before His seat
The bride of many members is before the One
The throne of the Father, the White Cloud of relief
The throne of the Father of the redeeming Son

There He is, there He is, HOLY, HOLY, HOLY
The cry from within and without
From the halls and down the streets
HOLY, HOLY, HOLY is the harmonious shout

About His throne fly four serving clouds
All lesser with only a messenger's voice
Each magnify and glorify each time around
They announce, proclaim and rejoice

One cries: the power of the White Cloud
One cries: the peace of the White Cloud
One cries: the all-knowing purpose of the White Cloud
One cries: the position of the sovereign White Cloud

Thunder comes from the throne
A voice is heard by all there
The fires of His aspect are known
But in His presence, all feel His care

Sitting on His throne and seen by all
Is the beautiful Lord of this heavenly place
For all come when they hear His call
Drawn by His power, love and grace

There is a sea akin to glass clear
In front of where the Father holds sway
The four serving clouds are always there
Now these four are heard to say

HOLY, HOLY, HOLY
LORD GOD ALMIGHTY
WHO WAS AND IS AND IS TO COME
And the twenty four start to speak

As they fall before the Father White Cloud
YOU ARE WORTHY O LORD
TO RECEIVE GLORY, HONOR AND POWER
FOR YOU CREATED ALL THINGS

BY YOUR WILL ALL EXIST AND ARE
How great and powerful the Father
Who sits on the throne before the bride
How glorious and supreme in every matter

There are the twenty-four
The four serving clouds are about
Around are the spirits of the Lord
All in worship and praise bow down

For the redeeming adoption goes forth
The time of both trouble and salvation comes
His plan is to redeem and save the earth
Through the Lordship of the Blue Cloud Son

The White Cloud, the Father God
Sits with the scroll deed in His divine hand
On the scripts back are seven locks
This is the mortgage deed to the earth land

A great strong angelic cloud stands and proclaims
WHO IS WORTHY TO OPEN THE DEED
AND TO LOOSE ITS LOCKS give the name
For He is the One, the Lamb, the Seed

No one is seen or comes for a time
Over and on and under no one is found
To open the deed of this redemptive kind
To reclaim divinely the once lost ground

Sadness arises, but one of the twenty four says it loud
DO NOT WEEP; THE LION OF JUDAH,
THE ROOT OF DAVID HAS PREVAILED
AND WILL OPEN THE SCROLL'S LOCKS

In the midst of the Father's throne
Surrounded by the four serving clouds
In the midst of the elders, He is alone
Standing royal and announcing loud

The Lamb who once was slain
The Lamb with the Seven Spirits of God
The Lamb who comes and makes plain
That He is the Lamb worthy of laud

He takes the deed from Father's right hand
The Royal Son will take the world back
He is the One to relieve the lot of man
The One to quell the dark cloud's attack

He stands for all to see
A marvelous and wonderful One to all
The four clouds and the elders fall to their knees
And sing to Him a new song's call

They are there who hold a harp and a bowl,
This holds the prayers of the saints
YOU ARE WORTHY TO TAKE THE SCROLL
TO OPEN ITS LOCKS; FOR YOU WERE SLAIN

AND HAVE REDEEMED US TO GOD
BY YOUR BLOOD FROM EVERY TRIBE
AND EVERY TONGUE AND EVERY PEOPLE
AND HAVE MADE US KINGS

AND PRIESTS TO OUR FATHER GOD
AND WE SHALL REIGN ON THE EARTH
Many clouds, the four clouds and the twenty and four
Praise the Son for He is the Lord

WORTHY IS THE LAMB WHO WAS SLAIN
TO RECEIVE POWER AND RICHES
AND WISDOM AND STRENGTH AND HONOR
AND GLORY AND BLESSING

All saved creation above, on and under sing
BLESSING AND HONOR AND GLORY
AND POWER BE TO HIM WHO SITS
ON THE THRONE AND TO THE LAMB

FOREVER AND EVER! And the elders
Fall to their knees and praise
Their King and Lord, the Son of the Father
The Lamb, the Prince, the Ancient of Days

The locks are soon found open
The time comes for His wrath
Each lock, an aspect to finish sin
Ushering in the eternity of the Son's path

The first lock is opened and there now rides
A leader with a false peace for all
For he brings and offers an angry chide
Come and see as he hatefully calls

The second lock is opened and battle struts out
A cause, a reason, a rhyme, a war
Quickly! Your arms and weapons he shouts
Come see what you have in store

The third lock is opened and famine is now
For after war, economy always goes
All the earth for bread will readily bow
Come see the hunger the earth will know

The fourth lock is opened and death appears
Followed by his friend who is the grave
After war and want can death not leer?
Come see those who won't be saved

The fifth lock is opened and a cry is heard
The cry is from those who are slain
They are martyred everyone in turn
Come and see their love for God made plain

They loudly cry, HOW LONG, O LORD
HOLY AND TRUE UNTIL YOU JUDGE
AND AVENGE OUR BLOOD
ON THOSE WHO DWELL ON THE EARTH

They are told rest for a time and no more roam
Wear your robe of purest white
Others must walk your hard path home
Come see as others will see His light

The sixth lock is opened and the earth shakes
On the ground and in the first heaven's sky
The pitch and roll from this convulsing quake
Causes many through fear to desire to die

The sun goes black and the moon becomes red
Stars plummet; both mighty men and slaves feel fear
Everyone prays and begs only to be dead
The Lamb's anger and wrath appears

THE GREAT DAY OF HIS WRATH HAS COME
AND WHO IS ABLE TO STAND
It is the time of the Kingship of the Royal Son
His aspect is terrible in a sinful land

There is a scene from the martyred crew
Four new angelic clouds hold back the wind's blow
'Til another cloud says relent to gather a few
No harm to any until God's mark is bestowed

Twelve thousand from Judah
Twelve thousand from Reuben
Twelve thousand from Gad
Twelve thousand from Asher

Twelve thousand from Naphtali
Twelve thousand from Manasseh
Twelve thousand from Simeon
Twelve thousand from Levi

Twelve thousand from Issachar
Twelve thousand from Zebulun
Twelve thousand from Joseph
Twelve thousand from Benjamin

They are not alone wearing the white robe
Another number large and great
Are present to stand before the Lamb's throne
Never again to feel evil's pain and hate

SALVATION BELONGS TO OUR GOD
They hold palm branches and praise the King
WHO SITS ON THE THRONE, TO THE LAMB
This is the joyful song they sing

All around, the clouds and the four clouds
The twenty-four elders fall on their face
Worshiping their God and saying so proud
AMEN! BLESSING, GLORY AND WISDOM

THANKSGIVING, HONOR, POWER AND MIGHT
BE TO OUR GOD FOREVER AND EVER. AMEN
The ones who are in robes so white
Are victorious through the evil wrath of night

Forever they serve the Lamb alone
He will wipe away all their tears
The Royal Son from amid God's throne
Cares and leads and as the Shepherd appears

These one hundred and forty four thousand
And a number no one can count
Will not serve the dark cloud in an evil land
They died to stand upon the Lord's mount

The seventh lock is opened and all is still
For a time, silence is all any hear
Seven serving clouds stand following God's will
Another serving cloud has a divine censer

His incense rises with the prayers of the band
He fills the censer with the White Cloud's fire
He throws it down to the evil corrupt land
The seven stand with horns announcing the pyre

The death pyre is coming to the earth
There for the dead and the dying
On this death pyre there is no dearth
Of the dead, the dying and those left crying

The first horn blares and now comes the hail
With fire burning and smashing the lack of green
And after the green is assailed
Then there is little left for man to glean

The second horn blares; harm to the sea
Its life form and substance is gone
The explosion corrupts and does not let it be
Evil makes the world's everything go wrong

The third horn blares and the rivers are bitter
Men find sickness in their very being
The wormwood infects and makes them suffer
For corrupt are the rivers and the springs

The fourth horn blares and all feel the divine might
The sun, moon and stars are made obscure
From the sky, an announcing cloud is in sight
And cries out the decree from the Son so pure

The announcing cloud cries loudly, WOE, WOE,
He cries, WOE TO THE INHABITANTS OF
THE EARTH BECAUSE OF THE REMAINING
HORNS OF THE MESSENGERS READY TO BLOW

The fifth horn blares and the pit is open
Tormenting hordes are roused to be
They hurt and inflict the sinful men
For the destroyer is here for all to see

The sixth horn blares and the river dries
Armies are loose and come to kill
All of those that from this did not die
Still would not bow to the White Cloud's will

With one more divine horn to sound,
A mighty cloud comes from above with a bow
With a small book, he stands on both sea and ground
The words are sealed, but in time one will know

The cloud swears by the Royal Blue Son
The secret of the White Cloud is not light
For all that is promised will be done
God's will is powerful, just and right

The small book is righteous, good and here
For the wrath comes to show the way
The book tells of the dead, the dying and the tear
It is bittersweet relating the Lord's great day

There is a display as two men rise
They carry the Lord's hammer so high
They are hated for they see through holy eyes
The Lord's task is completed before they die

They tell, show and demonstrate the Son
The dark cloud seeks them out
They fall when their report is done
The whole evil world will give a shout

This gross act is a time for gala and glee
The two are dead and evil has ease
They will not stay dead and will again be
The darkness trembles and finds no peace

The two arise and go up high
A few see the reality of the Lord
He is greater than the death and the cry
He is greater than the dark and the sword

The seventh horn blares in glorious aspect
THE KINGDOMS OF THIS WORLD
HAVE BECOME THE KINGDOMS
OF OUR LORD AND HIS CHRIST

HE SHALL REIGN FOREVER AND EVER
The elders fall to worship God
WE GIVE YOU THANKS, O LORD GOD
THE ONE WHO IS, WAS AND IS TO COME

BECAUSE YOU HAVE TAKEN
YOUR GREAT POWER AND REIGNED,
THE NATIONS WERE ANGRY
AND YOUR WRATH HAS COME

AND THE TIME OF THE DEAD
THAT THEY SHOULD BE JUDGED
AND THAT YOU SHOULD REWARD
YOUR SERVANTS THE PROPHETS

AND THE SAINTS AND THOSE WHO FEAR
YOUR NAME, SMALL AND GREAT
AND SHOULD DESTROY THOSE
WHO DESTROY THE EARTH

The place opens and the ark is seen
For powerful is the work of the Lord
His word is sharp and so very keen
His word is as acute and like a sword

For in His temple there is right
For in His ark there is safety
For in His promise there is might
And all shake as these things be

A sign from the Father above in the sky
A WOMAN WITH CHILD IS NOW SEEN TO BE
The sign of a nation and a Lord to draw nigh
The history of redemption for all to see

The dark cloud first deceives up there
He takes a third with him in defeat
And is cast down with earth as his lair
To destroy the woman is his attempted feat

The child, the Lord went up and away
And the woman is driven to hide
A time, times and a half of mortal days
She will survive and she will strive

The dark cloud no longer is up there
He hurts the woman and others around
He loses to the child attempting his snare
He seeks to destroy everyone found

During his attacking bent, from the sea
A beast arises displaying both power and sin
Serving evil, aside the dark cloud he will be
His rule with darkness now to begin

The dark cloud anoints this beast to rule
Earth will consider him to be their god
The beast is part of the dark and cruel
The deluded earth offers him their laud

Yet another rises to complete the three
Imitating the real the darkness will try
Like a truth he attempts always to be
But in God's truth he will always deny

We have the darkness, the rule and the priest
They try to usurp the Father, Son and Servant
In the end, God's truth cause the false to desist
Truth accomplishes when false lies can't

For a time and times and half a time
Their lie will rule and lead most astray
Their error so great and of the kind
That draws the earth from God's only way

On a mount stand the martyred ones
The one hundred forty-four thousand
The pure and chaste that serve the Son
Chosen to take His call to all the land

They sing their song while others look on
Only they through their lives are worthy to sing
For only this number can learn this song
Redeemed and chosen by the holy King

THESE ARE THE ONES WHO WERE
NOT DEFILED WITH WOMEN, VIRGINS
THESE, WHO FOLLOW THE LAMB
WHEREVER HE GOES

THEY WERE REDEEMED FROM MEN
FIRSTFRUITS TO GOD AND THE LAMB
AND NO DECEIT WAS FOUND
HAVING NO FAULT BEFORE GOD

A soaring cloud declares the message to all
And announces all need to fear God
Another declares that the harlot will fall
She has given in to the deceiving sinful prod

A third follows saying to the earth so loud
Not to follow or accept the unholy three
Be humble before God and do not be proud
To follow evil leads to the tormenting sea

THEY SHALL ALSO DRINK
THE WINE OF THE WRATH OF GOD
WHICH IS POURED OUT FULL STRENGTH
INTO THE CUP OF HIS INDIGNATION

THEY SHALL BE TORMENTED WITH FIRE
BEFORE THE ANGELS AND THE LAMB
THE SMOKE WILL ASCEND FOREVER
THEY HAVE NO REST DAY OR NIGHT

WHOEVER WORSHIPS THE BEAST AND HIS IMAGE
WHOEVER RECEIVES THE MARK OF HIS NAME
But they who stand for God let them stand on
Keep the Lord's laws and believe in the Son

A voice calls from above and is heard to say
BLESSED ARE THE DEAD WHO DIE FROM
NOW ON IN THE LORD, THE SERVING SPIRIT
READILY AGREES THAT THEY MAY HAVE REST

FROM THEIR WORKS WHICH WILL FOLLOW
But they who stand for God let them stand on
Keep the Lord's laws and believe in the Son
Standing fast and loyal and remaining strong

Behold in the heavens the Son of Man
Regal is the appearing of the Blue Cloud
Terrible is His wrath, a sickle in His hand
The time of harvesting sin's grapes is now

The crop is full of wickedness and sin
And judgment and wrath is deserved
Prince as your promised harvest begins
Hold nothing back through love's reserve

Your love was given for many a year
Father's grace a gift offered to everyone
And evil, with delight caused the tear
And turned many from you, dear Son

Soon the Father and Son's wrath is complete
Seven serving clouds have the last
Of His judgments which will defeat
The evil and make evil's time past

The victorious will sing their songs
They have overcome the unholy three
They sing to the One who made them strong
They sing to the One who helped them be

GREAT AND MARVELOUS ARE
YOUR WORKS LORD GOD
JUST AND TRUE ARE YOUR WAYS
O KING OF THE SAINTS

WHO SHALL NOT FEAR YOU, O LORD
AND GLORIFY YOUR NAME
FOR YOU ALONE ARE HOLY
FOR ALL NATIONS SHALL COME

AND WORSHIP BEFORE YOU
YOUR JUDGMENTS ARE SHOWN
The temple is seen to be open
And the last judgments begin

The temple is no longer open
For a time no one can go in
The wrath will judge men's sin
As the last judgments begin

The seven clouds stand with their bowl
Each an aspect of wrath on sinful man
Each show a judgment the Son bestows
Each show the conceit of men in every land

The first bowl finds men sore
But they continue evil
The second bowl finds the sea poor
And death has its fill

The third finds the bloody river
To repay the death of the just ones
The fourth finds men afire
But their blasphemy continues on

The fifth finds men in darkness
They feel sin's extreme pain
The sixth finds the great flow less
The kings' road is made plain

The dark and evil three
Call forth all their evil men
To a mount and a valley
They call the disciples of sin

The seventh bowl is cast from the air
And it is heard said, IT IS FINISHED
There is a shaking of the dark cloud's lair
The Lord's judgment is accomplished

The aspect of the harlot is seen
She works for the dark three
Against the White Cloud is her mean
She spreads her wares across all the sea

The three and their smaller group
Who are led in the service of evil
Will turn and finish off the harlot
And they will have their fill

The three and their evil world
Turn and fight with the Lamb
The Royal Blue Cloud Righteous Word
Overcomes and His might will stand

The harlot is dead, no more to be
The start of defiance began with her
All heaven rejoices in the Lord's sovereignty
She corrupted many with her enticing lure

FOR THE HARLOT IS MADE DESOLATE
REJOICE OVER HER DEATH, O HEAVEN
AND YOU HOLY APOSTLES AND PROPHETS
FOR GOD HAS AVENGED YOU ON HER

THUS WITH VIOLENCE THE GREAT HARLOT
SHALL BE THROWN DOWN FOREVER
NO ARTISAN SHALL FIND HER ANYMORE
NO CRAFTSMAN SHALL FIND HER ANYMORE

NO LIGHT SHALL SHINE ON HER ANYMORE
NO WEDDINGS WILL BE AROUND HER ANYMORE
The great men were made fat by their lust
In her magic they placed their trust

IN HER WAS FOUND THE BLOOD OF THE SAINTS
AND ALL WHO WERE SLAIN OF EARTH
ALLEULUIA! SALVATION AND GLORY
BELONG TO THE LORD OUR GOD

The harlot is gone but the chaste bride waits
The marriage to the Royal Son is now
There comes the call, the divine dictate
For those to attend this wedding renowned

BLESSED ARE THOSE WHO ARE CALLED
TO THE MARRIAGE SUPPER OF THE LAMB
WORSHIP GOD! PROPHECY IS TESTIMONY
OF THE ROYAL BLUE CLOUD SON DIVINE

See the Royal One, He is peace
He rides the true white horse
HE IS CALLED FAITHFUL AND TRUE
RIGHTLY HE JUDGES AND MAKES WAR

HIS EYES ARE LIKE A FLAME OF FIRE
ON HIS HEAD ARE MANY CROWNS
HE WEARS A ROBE DIPPED IN BLOOD
HIS NAME IS THE WORD OF GOD

His army rides with their King
A chaste and pure army goes forth
For the King comes to a right thing
And takes evil and on evil makes war

He grabs and snatches and seizes
This earth that has gone astray
In His entire plan, He accomplishes
And He starts His kingdom stay

WHEN HE SPEAKS HIS WORDS ARE LIKE A SWORD
WITH WHICH HE STRIKES THE NATIONS
HE RULES THEM WITH A ROD OF IRON
HE TREADS THE WINEPRESS OF GOD'S WRATH

HE IS KING OF KINGS
HE IS LORD OF LORDS
He takes the evil beast
He takes the evil priest

Both are thrown in the tormenting lake
For they are two of the three
They are guilty of the evil prate
Forever in torment they will be

The others who followed the dark cloud
Die with the words the Blue Cloud say
Against God they chose to stand proud
God brings the proud low in His day

A cloud comes from Heaven above
He controls the prison and its seal
He is the instrument of the Dove
He seizes and shuts up the dark evil

HE LAYS HOLD OF THE DRAGON
THAT SERPENT OF OLD
WHO IS THE DEVIL AND SATAN
BINDING HIM A THOUSAND YEARS

The Kingdom has come
His time of earthly rule begins
The Kingdom of the Son
With no evil, with no sin

The Royal Blue Cloud
Sits on His throne
The Prince announces loud
And calls them who are His own

The chaste and pure bride is there
And those who made it through
They will rule under His care
For He rules in power and truth

After a thousand years
And for only a short time
The dark one gives out the spears
And deceives again and is unkind

The Royal Blue Cloud Prince Son
Declares enough and ends the strife
Now the dark cloud is finally done
He is tormented for all eternity's life

The dark evil is thrown into the lake
Where the blasphemous beast and priest are
This is the reward of all when evil they make
There is the reward when they follow rebellion's star

All who were find judgment
The White cloud's white throne is there
Death and the grave lose their bent
Residing forever in the lake of fire

The dark cloud of the evil
The followers and the other evil two
All of sin finds an eternal seal
For the King's wrath is through

SEE A NEW HEAVEN AND A NEW EARTH
THE FIRST HEAVEN, THE FIRST EARTH
PASSES AWAY, THERE IS NO MORE SEA
THE HOLY CITY, THE NEW JERUSALEM

COMING FROM HEAVEN MADE BY GOD
THE TABERNACLE OF GOD IS WITH MEN
HE DWELLS WITH THEM, THEY ARE HIS
HE IS WITH THEM AND IS THEIR GOD

GOD WIPES AWAY THE TEAR
THERE IS NO MORE DEATH
NOR SORROW, NOR CRYING, NOR PAIN
THE FORMER THINGS PASS AWAY

HE SITS ON HIS THRONE
HE MAKES ALL THINGS NEW
HE IS THE ALPHA, THE OMEGA
HE IS THE BEGINNING, THE END

HE BRINGS HIS REWARD
HE IS THE ALPHA, THE OMEGA
HE IS THE BEGINNING, THE END
HE IS THE FIRST, THE LAST

The King is a divine might
The Royal Blue Cloud is power
The Son is a saving light
The Prince is a strong tower

The Lamb gives His all
The Shepherd guides His own
The Almighty God stands tall
Forever He sits on His throne

The Savior saves
The Healer heals
The Grace gives
The Assuring Blood seals

The White Cloud rules the earth
His Son by His side for eternity
The earth redeemed and without dearth
All is accomplished that is to be

The earth is divinely restored back
And is set on the Lord's path
The evil is gone with his attack
Purged by the Lord's just wrath

HE SENDS HIS MESSENGER TO TESTIFY
THESE THINGS IN THE ASSEMBLIES
HE IS THE ROOT AND OFFSPRING
THE BRIGHT AND MORNING STAR

THE SPIRIT AND THE BRIDE SAY COME!
LET HIM WHO HEARS SAY COME!
LET HIM WHO DESIRES DRINK
OF THE FREE WATER OF LIFE

The Father and Son reside here below
These Clouds of a divine hue
And they who have had grace bestowed
And have believed in the Son so true

The White Cloud reigns supreme
With the Royal blue Prince Cloud
The Lamb once slain, now the King
For God lives, rules and is crowned

HE IS THE ALPHA, THE OMEGA
HE IS THE BEGINNING, THE END
HE IS THE FIRST, THE LAST
He is the victor over sin.

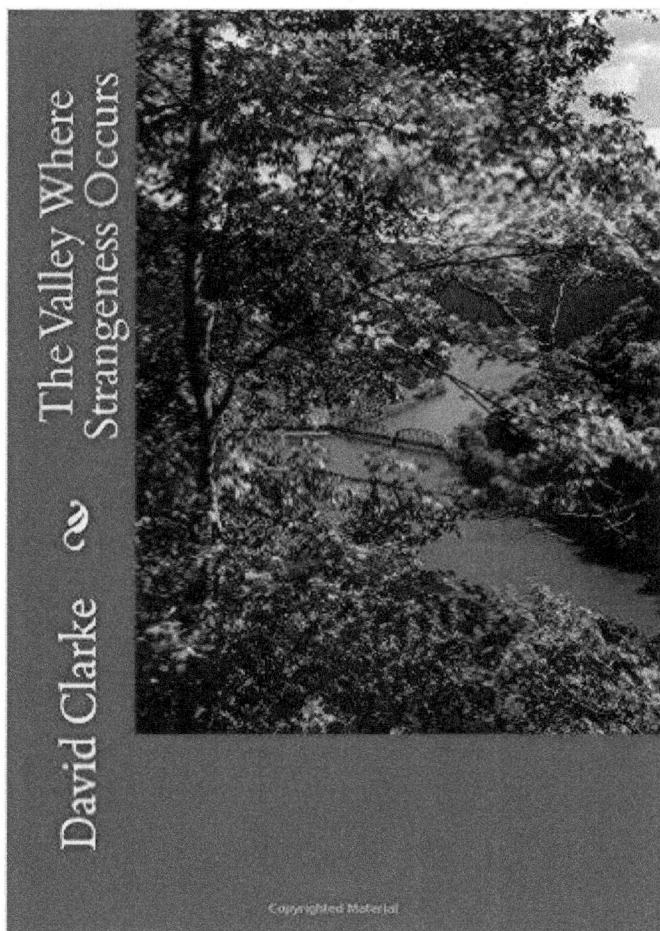

The Valley Where Strangeness Occurs

David Clarke

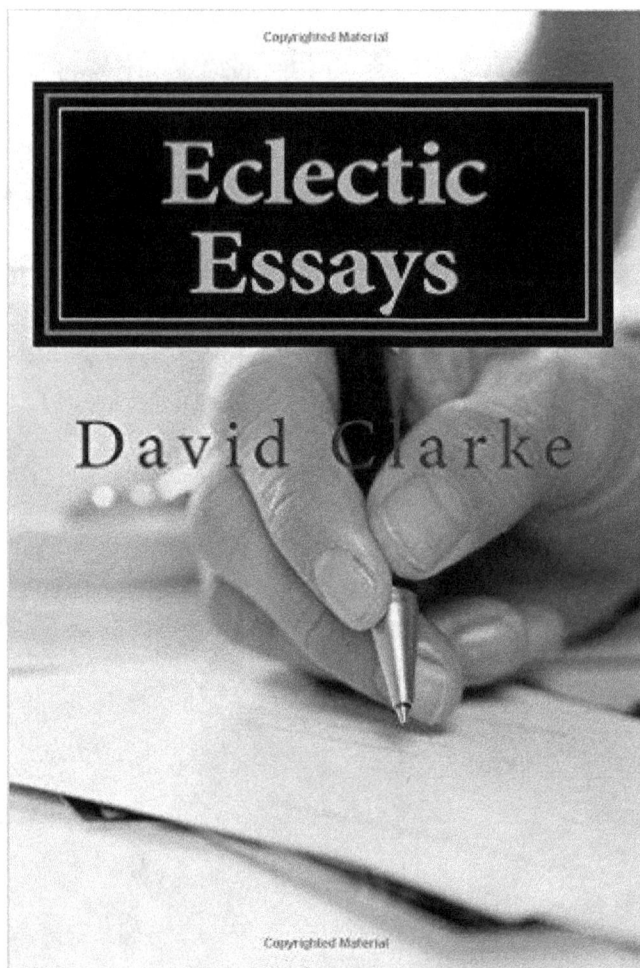

CONCERNING
THE CHRIST

DAVID E. CLARKE

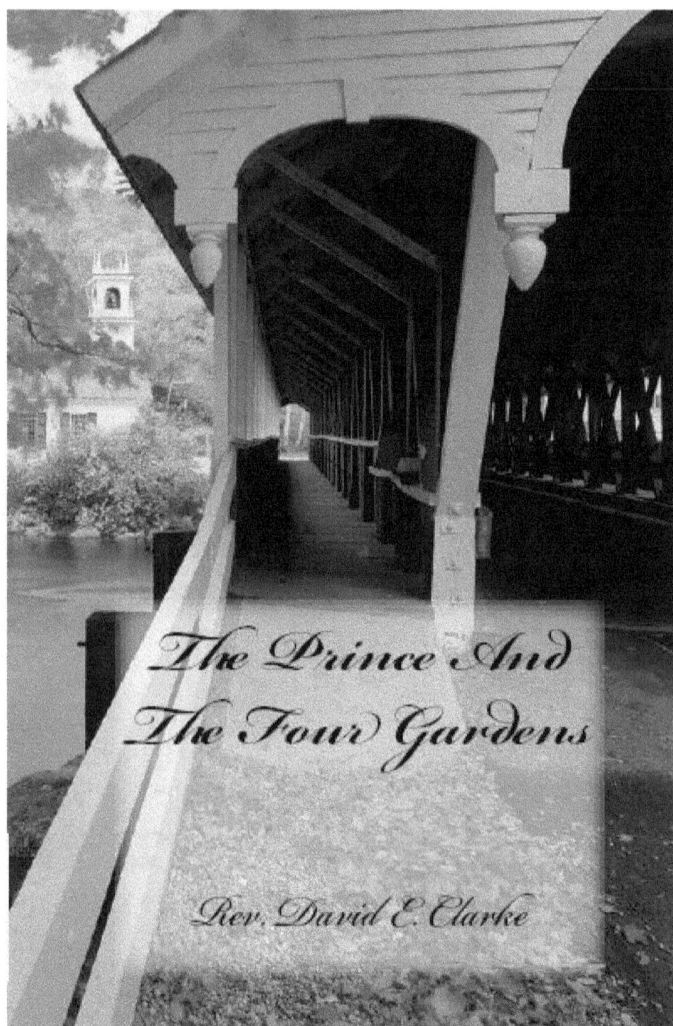

The Prince And
The Four Gardens

Rev. David E. Clarke

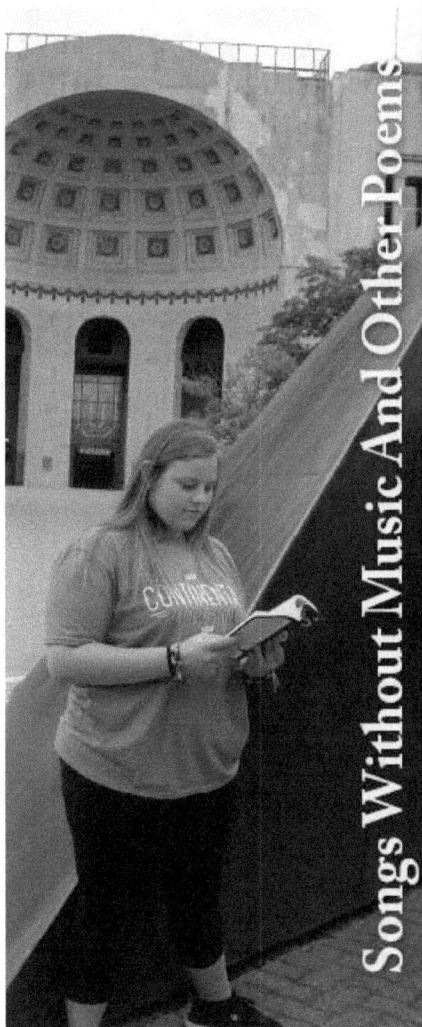

Songs Without Music And Other Poems

Rev. David E. Clarke

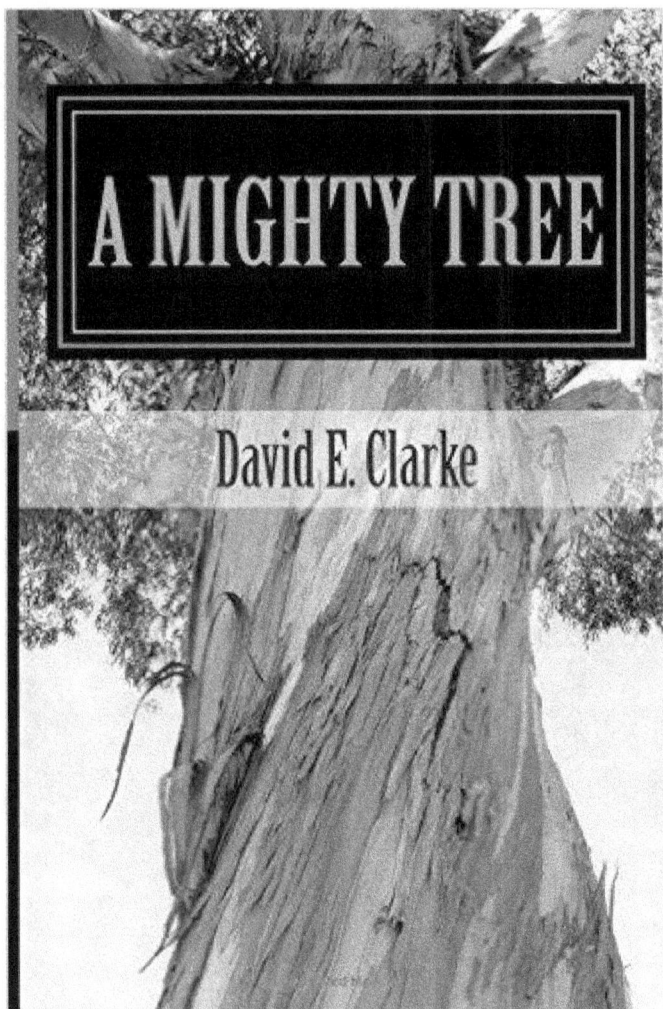

A MIGHTY TREE

David E. Clarke